D0787379

A LORD MUSEUM BOOK

STONES, BONES

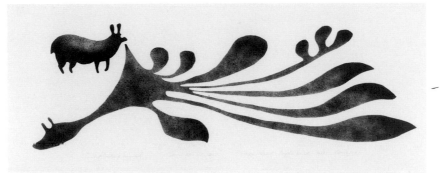

and STITCHES

STORYTELLING THROUGH INUIT ART

SHELLEY FALCONER and SHAWNA WHITE

TUNDRA BOOKS

To Sam, Sarah, and Josh, with love.
S.F.

For Jacob and Hannah, my own little storytellers.
S.W.

Copyright © 2007 by McMichael Canadian Art Collection

Museum Edition

Published in Canada by Tundra Books,
75 Sherbourne Street, Toronto, Ontario M5A 2P9

Published in the United States by Tundra Books of Northern New York,
P.O. Box 1030, Plattsburgh, New York 12901

Library of Congress Control Number: 2006909812

Library and Archives Canada Cataloguing in Publication

Falconer, Shelley
    Stones, bones and stitches : storytelling through Inuit art / Shelley Falconer, Shawna White.

Published in cooperation with the McMichael Canadian Art Collection and LORD Cultural Resources Planning
and Management.

ISBN 978-0-88776-854-5

    1. Inuit art – Canada – Juvenile literature. 2. Inuit artists – Canada – Juvenile
literature. I. White, Shawna II. McMichael Canadian Art
Collection III. LORD Cultural Resources Planning and Management IV. Title.

E99.E7F248 2007   j704.03'9712071   C2006-904067-2

We acknowledge the financial support of the Government of Canada through
the Book Publishing Industry Development Program (BPIDP) and that of the
Government of Ontario through the Ontario Media Development Corporation's
Ontario Book Initiative. We further acknowledge the support of the Canada Council
for the Arts and the Ontario Arts Council for our publishing program.

ONTARIO ARTS COUNCIL
CONSEIL DES ARTS DE L'ONTARIO

Text Design: Terri Nimmo

Printed in China

1 2 3 4 5 6   12 11 10 09 08 07

CONTENTS

Beaufort Sea

ALASKA

● Tuktoyaktuk
● Inuvik
Aklavik ●
● Paulatuk

YUKON
TERRITORY

*Great
Bear Lake*

NUNA

● Whitehorse

NORTHWEST
TERRITORIES

● Yellowknife
*Great
Slave Lake*

C A N A D

BRITISH
COLUMBIA

ALBERTA

SASKATCHEWAN

M

ELLESMERE ISLAND

KALAALLIT NUNAAT
(Greenland)

60°

Baffin Bay

Davis Strait

BAFFIN ISLAND

Iglulik *(Igloolik)*

Cumberland Sound

SOUTHAMPTON ISLAND

Korok Inlet

Iqaluit *(Frobisher Bay)*

Labrador Sea

Qamanittuaq *(Baker Lake)*

Kinngait
(Cape Dorset)

TUJJAAT *(Nottingham Island)*

Ungava Bay

NUNAVIK

Puvirnituq
(Povungnituk)

Inukjuak

Hudson Bay

LABRADOR

49°

James Bay

NEWFOUNDLAND

QUEBEC

A

ONTARIO

PRINCE EDWARD ISLAND

NEW BRUNSWICK

NOVA SCOTIA

This LORD Museum Book is part of a series published by Tundra Books in collaboration with LORD Cultural Resources Planning and Management and the museums themselves.

LORD MUSEUM BOOKS

LORD Museum Books are designed to help you experience museum stories to treasure from around the world. When you pick up a book, you make connections between the words, the pictures, and the story that unfolds as you read. When you visit a museum, you make connections too – connections between different kinds of objects from clothing, paintings, music, fossils, machines, and whole buildings – to reveal a multitude of stories from real life. In many museums you can even get to listen, touch, smell, and join in activities that help reveal the stories behind the objects.

Stones, Bones and Stitches exhibits work from the McMichael Canadian Art Collection in Kleinburg, Ontario, Canada. The gallery's responsibility is to collect, preserve, and present artwork and information so that we can all share in the stories of the past. Every gallery and museum has different stories to discover, depending on the objects it collects. What all museum objects have in common is that they are real things that help us to connect what happened in the past with how things work today. LORD Museum Books bring museums and the fascinating information they contain right to you so that you can enjoy them whenever you want, whether or not you have the chance to visit in person.

READER'S NOTE

Crossed-referenced words and phrases appear in italics.

INTRODUCTION

I grew up in a home where art, history, books, and museums were the *stuff* of everyday life. Through the mysticism of a Lawren Harris landscape, the horror of a Goya scene, the poeticism of an Ozias Leduc still life, and the tortured interior of a Van Gogh, my young mind was free to wander, explore, and discover. Art can tell us powerful stories – stretching the imagination and reminding us of who we are, and what we can be. As a grown-up, I've spent these last few years working with one of Canada's most significant collections of Canadian art: the McMichael Canadian Art Collection. This important collection has allowed me to wander through the many stories of our country's varied landscape. With a particular focus on the Far North, my colleague, Shawna White, and I look forward to sharing with you some of the magic of the North's imaginary landscapes and indigenous communities. This visual journey will interweave some of Canada's most prominent Inuit artists with their artworks, stories, and culture so you, too, can wander, explore, and discover.

Shelley Falconer, director of exhibitions and programs and senior curator
Shawna White, assistant curator
McMichael Canadian Art Collection
Kleinburg, Ontario

ACKNOWLEDGEMENTS

The authors wish to acknowledge the vision and foresight of Barbara Tyler and Jean Blodgett, without whom this book would not be possible.

Special recognition is due to Gail Dexter Lord and Noreen Taylor for their support in the development of this publication. We would also like to sincerely thank Karen Williamson, Sharona Adamowicz-Clements, Janine Butler, and Linda Morita for their expertise and assistance.

OVILOO TUNNILLIE

WOMAN QUARRYING STONE

I have always been fascinated by rocks for as long as I can remember, probably because I would make things out of soapstone later in my life.

Oviloo Tunnillie in *Inuit Women Artists*, 1994

OVILOO TUNNILLIE *(E7-779)*

Born in 1949, Oviloo Tunnillie grew up in Kangia, a camp outside of *Kinngait (Cape Dorset)* on Baffin Island. When she was only seven or eight years old, Oviloo became ill with *tuberculosis* and was sent away to a hospital in Quebec City for more than three years. This early exposure to sickness, hardship, and loneliness inspired many of her more powerful works. Once Oviloo returned to her family, her father taught her how to carve stone. At the age of seventeen, she carved her first sculpture. After the death of her father a few years later, Oviloo began to take carving seriously.

Since 1972, Oviloo has been creating sculpture and experimenting with form, materials, and subject matter. Today, she is recognized as one of the *North's* most skilled sculptors. Her work tells us much about the changing world of the Inuit – from traditional experiences to the impact of modern life on the Inuit – and often brings out feelings of tragedy, sorrow, and joy. Oviloo's sculpture is featured in important collections across Canada.

WOMAN QUARRYING STONE

For me, the story or idea behind my sculpture is more important than the actual technique. That's what I want people to see when they look at my work. The story is more serious to me than actually making the piece.

Oviloo Tunnillie in *Northern Rock*, 1999

This moving and powerful sculpture reveals the emotion and hardship experienced by the Inuit woman sculptor. The elderly woman reaches outward from the stone mass, demanding our empathy, respect, and sorrow.

Woman Quarrying Stone
Korok Inlet serpentinite, 55.0 x 22.0 x 45.5 cm

It didn't make sense to me to carve scenes of traditional life because I was not there so I began to carve from my own experiences – both happy and sad. . . . Because I am a woman who has always worked with stone, I did this sculpture of the woman carrying stone on her back. It's really more about working with stone in general than specifically about quarrying. I do like sculpture that has unfinished parts like this one.

Oviloo Tunnillie in *Northern Rock*, 1999

This contemporary work by Oviloo combines the past with the present to tell about the difficulties faced by many women sculptors today. The heaviness of the stone, the harsh conditions, and the danger of the quarries are embodied in a work that shows us less about the old way of life and more about a culture that is changing and emerging.

Oviloo's artistic practice and work is part of a long tradition passed down through generations of Inuit. Many years of poor hunting in the 1930s led to widespread starvation among Inuit. In 1939, the Supreme Court of Canada ruled that Inuit were entitled to the same health, education, and social services as Indians were granted in the 1876 Indian Act. The Canadian government began relocating Inuit to permanent settlements, forever changing their traditional nomadic lifestyle. Officials and other visiting individuals from the South began to recognize the unique carving skills of the Inuit. Artist James Houston first visited Arctic Quebec and brought back carvings with him to Montreal. Members of the Canadian Handicraft Guild liked what they saw and began collecting and exhibiting the works Houston brought back. He was eventually hired by the Federal Department of Indian Affairs and Northern Development to be responsible for the development of the arts and crafts programs in the North.

Beginning in the 1940s, Inuit expanded upon their traditional carving skills – used to make tools, weapons, small toys, and religious objects – to produce what we know today as Inuit sculpture.

Korok Inlet Serpentinite

Soapstone (talc steatite) is the common term often used to describe the stone used in Inuit sculpture. It is very soft and can be easily carved with little more than a fingernail. Although the type of stone used varies from community to community, serpentinite and serpentine, which are harder than soapstone, are more commonly used in Inuit art.

Quarrying

I haven't gone down to the quarry site for many years now. My husband goes down to Kangisukutaq to get stone, but he rarely carves. I like the stone that comes from the bottom area, deep underground, rather than the stone that is near the surface.

Oviloo Tunnillie in Northern Rock, 1999

Quarrying stone in the Arctic is a very complex and dangerous process. The majority of sculptors use stone from their own regions, but finding the quarrying sites and getting the stone out of the ground are both time-consuming and costly. For Kinngait artists such as Oviloo, finding stone is a difficult journey by boat to one of three quarry sites. The stone used in this sculpture is serpentinite from the relatively new Kangisukutaq quarry in Korok Inlet, an eight-hour trip east of Kinngait.

Quarrying is often done in the winter, as it is easier to haul the stone by sled over frozen water and snow-covered land. Sometimes the stone is dug up in the summer and then left until the wintertime to transport back. Finding the right stone is crucial. It must not contain any cracks because these will split during carving and ruin the sculpture. The rock should also have an even density and shouldn't be too hard or too soft.

Stone is removed from the ground with sledgehammers, crowbars, and steel wedges. Dynamite cannot be used, as the explosion will damage the stone. The quarries are dangerous places, and injuries are common. A young carver named Jutani Parr was killed in 1998 when a rock overhang collapsed and crushed him.

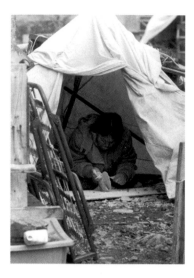

Carving

I have to start thinking a few days, or even weeks, ahead about what I am going to make. Sometimes I don't use a particular stone for quite a while because I am thinking about what I can make out of it. I don't draw anything on paper beforehand. I just start working on the stone when I know what I am going to make.

Oviloo Tunnillie in *Northern Rock*, 1999

Artists usually work outdoors while carving because of the great amount of dust. Some sculptors work in small tents or shacks constructed just outside their houses, which provide a degree of shelter. Sculpting is a year-round activity, and many artists can be found working outside even when the temperature is -25°C (-13°F)!

The process begins by roughly blocking out the desired shape using a hammer and chisel. Areas of stone are then slowly removed from the blocked-out form using a variety of tools such as rasps and files until the desired shape is achieved. The finishing stage includes sanding the sculpture and in some cases providing a wax coating to increase shine. Works are then purchased by the local co-operative, who then sell the pieces through a large network of galleries and dealers in the South.

KINNGAIT (CAPE DORSET)

Kinngait is located on the southwest coast of Baffin Island. With about thirteen hundred residents, Kinngait is home to the largest number of artists in the Arctic, with almost one-quarter of the labour force actively working as artists. Kinngait means "mountains" in English.

In 1957, James Houston initiated the first printmaking experiments in Kinngait. These early prints were sold through the Hudson's Bay Company in Winnipeg. The Hudson's Bay Company had long been involved in the North, having set up various trading posts as early as 1717 along the west coast of Hudson Bay.

E7-779

Traditionally, Inuit only went by first names. In the 1940s, the Canadian government conducted a census of Inuit and changed how individuals were identified for government records. Each Inuit was assigned a number and given a stamped disc looped on a sturdy string to wear. *E* stood for east and *W* stood for west. Early Inuit sculpture often was signed on the bottom with the disc number of the artist. By the late 1960s, this system was phased out, replaced by Project Surname. Surnames that were chosen at this time often were those of a father or relative who had passed away. For example, Kenojuak and her husband, Johnniebo, adopted his father's name, Ashevak, as their surname.

THE NORTH

Generally, the North refers to communities located above the 60th parallel of latitude on a map. Likewise, reference to the South means communities south of the 60th parallel of latitude.

A NOTE ABOUT PLACE NAMES

The North has fascinated explorers around the world since the sixteenth century. Many expeditions were undertaken to explore the region, most notably the numerous attempts to discover the so-called Northwest Passage – a sea passage through the Arctic providing a shortcut to the Far East. Non-Inuit names were assigned to various regions with each expedition. It is now becoming common to use the Inuit names for these communities. For example, Cape Dorset is now known as Kinngait, although you will still see the name Cape Dorset used in some instances.

TUBERCULOSIS

Tuberculosis (TB) is one of the world's most common and deadly diseases. It is a bacterial infection that mostly affects the lungs and is easily spread through the air when an infected person sneezes or coughs. In the past, TB was referred to as consumption.

In this small boat the people are cramped together as they want to live – always to face death.

Joe Talirunili in *Joe Talirunili: A Grace Beyond the Reach of Art*, 1977

JOE TALIRUNILI (E9-818)

Joe Talirunili was a well-known artist and storyteller from *Puvirnituq*, Nunavik (Arctic Quebec). He was born at Neahungnik Camp (which means "headache" in English), about fifty kilometres (31 miles) north of Puvirnituq. It is difficult to determine exactly when he was born. Government records state 1893, but Joe himself claims 1906 as his birthdate. For most of his life, Joe lived with his family on the land. His father's name was Putugu (big toe) and his mother's was Puala (mitten). Joe travelled by boat with other members of his family as they moved from camp to camp when the seasons changed. On one of those trips, the boat was destroyed, and about forty people drowned. Events like this, along with his experiences living on the land, provided Joe with the main inspiration for his work. Joe sculpted and drew scenes of camp life; the hunt and his famous *migration* carvings were repeated many times in his work. Joe had two wives, the second of whom was named Lydia Paniakpik. Together they had five children, but two died. Joe died on September 11, 1976.

Technically, Joe was not considered a great carver, as his work is often crude and somewhat clumsy. This may be due partly to an injury he received at the age of nineteen when his father accidentally shot him in the right arm. Refusing to have the arm removed, Joe pushed it back in place and bound it with seal fat, some skin from the stomach of a fox, and whale skin. The arm never healed properly and was a constant source of pain for him throughout his life.

THE MIGRATION

Who are these people crammed into this boat? Where are they going?

JOE TALIRUNILI

THE

MIGRATION

The Migration
Stone and sealskin with wood, 32.5 x 42.0 x 23.0 cm

Can you imagine a journey such as this? Travelling in a boat with no motor? This is exactly how Joe Talirunili travelled as a young child with his entire family (some forty people), along with their belongings. The journeys were long and hard. Someone would have to be on constant lookout for large pieces of ice and for storms that may be forming in the distance.

What a tremendous story is told through this work. Also known as *Joe's Boat, The Migration* tells a tale of hardship, endurance, and perseverance. It is a story of survival. In search of better hunting grounds, a group of Inuit sought to leave the mainland. They had to work quickly to build an *umiak* before the ice span on which they were stranded broke apart. Joe relates the story as follows:

> The umiak was entirely hand-made with no nails, but just rope. It probably took four sets of kayaks and probably sixty sealskins to make the umiak. The men and the women were constantly working day and night in order to finish the umiak before the ice had all melted, which was their only land. . . . These people went through a really rough time, fear of the ice melting and not finishing the umiak on time. (Joe Talirunili in *Joe Talirunili: A Grace Beyond the Reach of Art*, 1977)

Joe goes on to say that when the umiak was finished, a tremendous thunderlike crash filled the air and frightened the children. Large chunks of ice were melting and smashing together with a great roar. The movement of the ice also left a clear path for the Inuit to follow. Setting off in search of land, the Inuit sailed the umiak through the icy-cold waters. The group would drift for almost two months. At one point, as they were approaching land, it appeared as if the land were moving away. Joe's grandmother said, "The land is moving away and leaving us behind." Amitok, Joe's uncle, suggested that they shoot at the land to bring them closer. His shot hit the side of a mountain, and soon they had reached the shore. The landing site was very steep, and a strong wind forced the people to stay in the umiak. For almost a week they could not move, and Joe recalls his mother saying that they might have to eat one another because they were so hungry! The weather changed soon after that, and the group was able to move onto the land.

Stone and Sealskin with Wood

Joe depicted several renditions of this frightening journey from his childhood. In this version, Joe's grandmother, Aulayuk, is the leader of the boat and stands behind the sail. Joe himself is depicted as an infant in the *amautik* of his mother, who is seated behind the mast. Joe could recall most of the names of everyone in the boat, although he varied the number of people in the boat from carving to carving. This version has forty people. In other carvings of this subject, the figures are removable, set in place like pegs in a board. This sculpture was carved out of a very soft grey stone found around Puvirnituq.

PUVIRNITUQ

Puvirnituq (formerly called Povungnituk) is located on the northeast coast of Hudson Bay, close to the migratory paths of caribou herds. About twelve hundred people call this place home. Puvirnituq means "the place that smells of rotten meat" in English. In 1958, the Povungnituk Sculptors Society was formed. Puvirnituq also developed a printing program similar to the one at Cape Dorset, and Joe was one of the first to be involved. Although the program was forced to shut down in 1989 because of financial difficulties, a new carving and printmaking studio opened in 2005.

MIGRATION

Inuit were once a semi-nomadic people travelling from camp to camp with the change of seasons and to find new sources of food. Traditional forms of transportation included the komatik (sled) pulled by dogs, kayak, and umiak.

UMIAK

An umiak is a large wood-frame boat covered with seal or walrus skin that typically holds thirty or more people. It is powered by paddles or oars and sometimes by a sail.

AMAUTIK

An amautik is a specially designed parka worn by Inuit women in the central and eastern Arctic that contains a pouch in the back to hold a baby. The babies were naked, and layers of grass or moss on the bottom of the pouch acted like a diaper. Children usually travelled by amautik until they reached the age of three.

STAMP DESIGN

One of Joe's migration carvings was used on a stamp in 1978 as part of the series Inuit – Travel by Canada Post.

NANOOK OF THE NORTH

In 1922, Robert J. Flaherty filmed *Nanook of the North* near Inukjuak, which is south of Puvirnituq. Although it was largely staged, it is considered to be the first full-length feature documentary film ever made. An Inuk named Allakariallak played the character of Nanook. Tragically, he starved to death while on a hunting trip two years after the film's release.

JESSIE OONARK

UNTITLED

JESSIE OONARK (E2-384)

Jessie Oonark's story is one of hardship, perseverance, and dignity. Born in 1906, just outside the community of *Qamanittuaq (Baker Lake)*, Jessie was given the name Una – meaning "this one" in *Inuktitut*. Growing up on a diet of caribou, fish, duck, and geese, she performed many traditional tasks with the *ulu*, a woman's knife, including the preparation of caribou skins for *summer tents* and lining for fur clothing. Sadly, Jessie and her mother lost her father at a young age. Raised by her uncle and her grandmother, she learned many skills from her elders. Surviving a harsh environment and long periods of starvation, Jessie had only a brief childhood. She married at the young age of eleven or twelve and around 1926 gave birth to the first of thirteen children.

Difficult times lay ahead as Jessie and her family continued to struggle with life on the land. In the 1950s, as hunting became increasingly difficult and *epidemics* swept through the camps, she lost her husband and three young children. Close to death in their *igloo*, Jessie and her young daughter were rescued by the RCMP and taken to Baker Lake for hospitalization. While there, Jessie met a biologist, Dr. Andrew Macpherson, who shared his paper and coloured pencils and encouraged her to draw. She was the first artist in Baker Lake to be asked to make drawings for sale.

By 1960, Jessie's artistic career began to unfold. Encouraged to apply her designs to clothing, she produced parkas, wall hangings, and kamiks (boots). The Canadian government provided her with a space to work and paid her a monthly salary to continue developing her creativity.

By the 1970s, her work was hanging in major Canadian galleries and museums, including the prime minister's office. Today, she is celebrated as one of Canada's most famous artists. Jessie's strong sense of identity and vision is shared through the many prints, drawings, and wall hangings found in collections around the world. Jessie's children – including

Untitled
Wool, felt, embroidery thread, thread, 120.2 x 130.3 cm

Victoria Mamnguqsualuk, Janet Kigusiuq, and William Noah – are also well-respected artists. Jessie died in 1985.

UNTITLED: WALL HANGING

This 1973 photograph captures the artist in her tiny, cramped house, commonly known as a *matchbox*. Seated on her bed, with sewing materials around her, Jessie is working on a wall hanging in her lap. Weaving together traditional sewing techniques and the language of art and design – shape, colour, space, and rich Inuit imagery – Jessie created some of Canada's most original and expressive works of art.

Intense colours, beautiful stitching, immense size, and brilliantly designed compositions are typical and important elements of Jessie's wall hangings. Her technique is rooted in the traditional Inuit sewing method of decorating for traditional skin clothing – designs cut from one fabric and appliquéd to another piece of fabric. Abstract shapes such as Y's, triangles, and circles are regularly used for symbolic and design purposes. In this wall hanging, Jessie also includes hearts. Much of her work draws on her extensive memory of Inuit stories, traditions, and wildlife. Birds, fish, caribou, the ulu, shamans, transformed creatures, and spirits provide vibrant clues to life in the North where nature and culture are magically united.

QAMANITTUAQ (BAKER LAKE)

Qamanittuaq is located at the northwest end of Baker Lake near the mouth of the Thelon River. About twelve hundred people live here in Nunavut's only inland community. Qamanittuaq means "where the river widens" in English. It is near the geographic centre of Canada, some 320 kilometres (200 miles) west of Hudson Bay.

INUKTITUT SYLLABIC SYSTEM

Before 1856, Inuit did not have a written language. Information, knowledge, and wisdom were passed down from generation to generation through storytelling. Missionaries to the North adapted the syllabic system that had been devised for the Cree language for use by Inuit. The first book translated into Inuktitut was the Bible.

ULU

An ulu is a multi-purpose crescent-shaped knife used by Inuit women. The ulu is still widely used today to cut meat, remove the hair from animal skins, and to cut clothing from hides.

EPIDEMICS IN THE ARCTIC

Infectious diseases, such as measles, brought over by Europeans had a devastating effect on the people of the Arctic. In the early nineteenth century, the population of the Western Arctic had been estimated at around twenty-five hundred people. By 1910, there were only one hundred and fifty people left alive. There were recurring epidemics and periods of starvation up to the 1950s.

In the Eastern Arctic, the effects of disease were more sporadic. The Sadlirmiut, a local group from Southampton Island, were completely wiped out by dysentery (a really horrible disease of the digestive tract), which they caught from sailors on the Scottish whaler *Active* during the winter of 1902–03.

TYPES OF HOUSING

Igloo

Constructed of thick, packed snow, igloos use the same design principles found in the great cathedrals of Europe. The dome shape is very sturdy and can withstand high winds. Igloos were mostly used as temporary shelter during long winter hunting trips.

Qarmaq (Sod House)

Qarmaqs were constructed by digging a hole into the ground around which were piled rocks and sod. Pieces of wood or whalebone were used as a frame for the roof, which was then covered with skins and sod. A raised platform was placed at the back for sleeping.

Tent

Summer living was traditionally in a tent constructed of caribou hides.

Matchbox House

Small, prefabricated housing units built by the Canadian government at various centralized locations, matchbox houses started appearing in the North in the 1950s.

LUKTAQIATSUK

OWL

SPIRIT

Making pieces like this is not as difficult as carving the stone blocks for printing.

Lukta Qiatsuk in *Northern Rock*, 1999

LUKTA QIATSUK (E7-1060)

Lukta Qiatsuk was born at a camp near Kinngait (Cape Dorset) in 1928. Although he cannot recall the name of the camp in which he was born, he does remember that he lived with his family for some time at Ikerrasak, the camp where fellow artist Kenojuak Ashevak was born. He is the son of Kiakshuk, another very important and well-respected artist. His wife, Pudloo, was also a sculptor, and their sons Pootoogook and Palaya are artists themselves.

Lukta spent much of his life living on the land and was a very skilled hunter. His exceptional skills as a carver, however, have gained him his distin-guished reputation. Lukta's work is represented in major institutions in Canada and has been featured on a Canadian postage stamp as part of the Native Nativity Series.

When printmaking was introduced into Kinngait, Lukta was one of the first to be involved. He moved there permanently in 1960. A master printmaker, Lukta contributed to almost all of the annual print collections from 1959 to 1980. He died in 2004.

OWL SPIRIT

Owl Spirit is a tale about transformations. It not only shows the union of walrus and owl, but also suggests the changes in Inuit life and culture that have happened over the past one hundred years or so. This large, magnificent piece is carved from the skull of a *bowhead whale* that washed ashore on *Tujjaat (Nottingham Island)* a century or two ago. Artist Toni Onley and printing co-op arts adviser Terry Ryan first discovered the whalebone lying on the beach in the summer of 1975 while they were

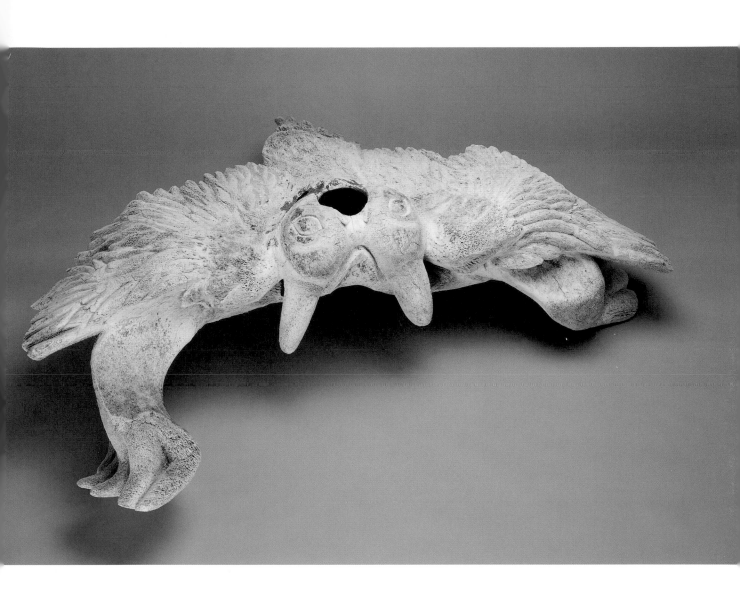

Owl Spirit
Whalebone, 46.0 x 156.8 x 103.5 cm

flying over the island. As the whalebone was too heavy to be taken by their plane at the time, a boat was sent for it the following year. It was given to Lukta Qiatsuk to carve.

Owl Spirit was carved in 1987. Working outside in the summer months, Lukta relied on his advanced carving skills to work the delicate bone by hand. Using the natural shape of the whalebone, Lukta carved away what did not belong, allowing the majestic forms of both walrus and owl to come through. Upon close examination of the work, one is awed by the power of the individual animals and by the skill of the artist who so beautifully carved them. Lukta was able to successfully transform the old, long-forgotten, and weatherworn whale skull into a treasured work of art that the McMichael is privileged to include in its collection.

Bowhead Whale Skull

For centuries, whalebone has been a valuable natural resource for Inuit. It is used for many purposes, including structural support for sod and stone houses, sled runners, tools, harpoon tips, and toys. Whale blubber is still eaten as a delicacy and was used as fuel for lamps. American and European *whalers* also relied heavily on the bowhead whale for baleen, which was used to manufacture buggy whips and parasol ribs, and to stiffen corsets. Because of their skills as hunters and seamstresses, hundreds of Inuit men and women were hired to work on the whaling ships. During this period, large quantities of manufactured goods entered into Inuit society and many Inuit were taken "on tour" to American cities. Since that time, Inuit culture has had to adapt to the changing realities around it. One such way was the development of the arts in the North, which transformed traditional skills into viable income-generating sources. It is this keen ability to transform and adapt that has allowed Inuit to survive in one of the harshest climates on the planet.

BOWHEAD WHALE (*BALAENA MYSTICETUS*)

Native to the Arctic waters, the bowhead whale grows to about eighteen metres (60 feet) in length and often weighs one hundred tons or more. It has the thickest blubber of any whale and possesses the longest and largest number of baleen plates (attached to the upper jaws and used by the whale to filter food), making it an ideal target for hunters.

TUJJAAT (NOTTINGHAM ISLAND)

Tujjaat (Nottingham Island) is 120 kilometres (75 miles) southwest of Cape Dorset. It has been uninhabited since October 1970, when residents migrated to larger settlements such as Kinngait. Tujjaat is home to a prominent walrus population.

Whalebone has to be aged between fifty and one hundred years before an artist is able to work with it because it is very oily and smelly!

WHALERS

In the 1850s, the North Atlantic commercial whaling industry began large-scale operations in the Arctic. Many whaling fleets were based on the East Coast at ports such as New Bedford and Sags Harbour. Whaling ships would sail around South America and head north into the Arctic. Whalers took vast quantities of bowhead whales from the area over the decades, causing great hardship for the Inuvialuit people living there. By 1905, the Arctic whale stocks had almost completely collapsed. Fortunately, 1905 also saw the invention of plastic, which brought to an end the exploitation of the whale for baleen.

ESKIMO

The term *Eskimo* was the commonly used name for Arctic cultural groups in Canada's North until 1977. It is, in fact, a derogatory term, coined by neighbouring First Nations groups in competition with them for territory and resources. Today, we use the term *Inuit*, which means "the people" and is the term Canadian Arctic peoples use to identify themselves.

ALLIOK

DAVIDRUBENPIQTOUKUN

My people are a storytelling society. Stories of hunting, travelling, people gatherings, hardships, humorous situations, death and birth are told to us in the comfort of a warm tent, after a hot meal. Inuit people are good listeners, as I have come to realize.

David Ruben Piqtoukun in his artist statement, *The Storytellers*,
The Koffler Gallery, 1988

DAVID RUBEN PIQTOUKUN (W3-1119)

David Ruben Piqtoukun was born in 1950 in a camp between the Mackenzie River delta and *Paulatuk*, Northwest Territories. He spent the earliest part of his childhood travelling from camp to camp with his parents, Billy Ruben (Esktak) and Bertha Thrasher (Kagun), and his brothers and sisters. His mother's grandfather was Apakark, a *shaman* who was well known for his ability to control the weather and travel to the moon.

At a young age, David was sent away to residential schools, first at Aklavik and then at Inuvik, both of which were far from his home. While at the schools, David was forbidden to speak *Inuviluktun*. It took him about two years to learn English, and he eventually lost the ability to speak his native tongue. While home on school breaks, David spent a lot of his time with his grandfather Billy Thrasher, who was a whaler in Tuktoyaktuk. David started carving at the age of twenty-two after visiting his brother Abraham Anghik Ruben, who is also a noted sculptor. David moved to Toronto in 1981 and currently lives on Lake Simcoe in Ontario. David travels back and forth to Paulatuk, where he continues to learn about his culture. He then transforms this knowledge into visual form, focusing much of his work on lost Inuit traditions.

ALLIOK

An *alliok* is an evil spirit. In this work, David brings to life one of the stories he heard as a child. As in most cultures, stories taught children lessons, warned of dangerous situations, or simply eased them into sleep. Elders Evik Ruben and Marion Green relate the story of the *alliok* as follows:

Alliok
Stone with bone and teeth, 38.0 x 39.0 x 11.5 cm

Alliok (reverse)

A very young couple was travelling in the winter time. They were travelling without a dog team, so he had to drag the sled carrying his pregnant wife. In transit, she gave birth to twins, whom they were unable to care for. She was too weak and sick to feed them properly, so they buried them in the snow and travelled on in search of the nearest settlement to get help and regain their health. As they travelled, demonic spirits entered the twins' souls and bodies. Their heads became very enlarged, their eyes wild, their teeth grew from ear to ear, and they had short arms and legs. To get about in the snow, they had to hop around and follow the sled tracks. When they caught up to the parents who had deserted them, the twins hopped in the air and crushed the heads of their mother and father. (*The Storytellers*, The Koffler Gallery, 1988)

In this carving, David dramatically illustrates the *alliok* story. Imagine this creature hopping through the snow in search of its prey! The figure is almost entirely a head, with short little legs sprouting out the bottom. A fearsome creature indeed, this *alliok* could devour you in one gulp with its wide rows of teeth. Carved into the face on the reverse of the sculpture are images of the mother and father who abandoned their young children. The head of what appears to be an owl peers out through its nose.

Brazilian Soapstone, Caribou Teeth, Ivory, African Wonderstone

The terms of the 1993 Nunavut Land Claim Agreement state that each and every Inuk is entitled to remove fifty cubic yards (38 cubic metres) of carving stone per year from Crown lands without a permit. Because he lives in the South, David is not able to freely harvest stone from the land and must purchase stones for his sculptures. Buying by the pound, he is able to obtain materials from all over the world, whether it be alabaster from Italy or African wonderstone and Brazilian soapstone, as was used for *Alliok*.

Brazilian soapstone is very soft and can be easily carved with a pocketknife. Once a work is finished, it can be cooked in a very hot oven (1000°C+, or 1832°F+), which hardens the stone.

David works with a variety of hand tools, such as chisels, saws, hatchets, files, rasps, and knives. He will also use power tools if needed to work the material.

When pieces of stone arrive in my studio they are in all different shapes and sizes and that's what determines the sculpture a lot of the time. I let the form create the sculpture. I start at one point and it creates a chain reaction. One subject creates another and the shape of the material determines the sculpture. Sometimes I try to find a material that has the right shape for that subject that I want to create.

David Ruben Piqtoukun in *Out of Tradition* exhibition catalogue,
Winnipeg Art Gallery, 1989

PAULATUK
Paulatuk is located on Darnley Bay, about 885 kilometres (550 miles) northwest of Yellowknife. It is a small settlement with just more than three hundred residents. Paulatuk means "place of coal" in English.

INUVILUKTUN
There are different dialects of Inuktitut, and the Inuit call themselves different names depending on which region they live in:

Western Canada – Inuvialuit

Eastern Canada – Inuit

Greenland – Kalaallit

Alaska – Yupik and Inupiat

Inspirations for my stone carvings and sculptures have been drawn from my Inuit background, which is rich in mythology, tradition and custom . . .
David Ruben Piqtoukun in his artist statement,
Canadian Sculpture Centre, February 2000

SHAMAN RETURNING FROM THE MOON

In *Shaman Returning from the Moon*, David reaches back into his past for a new interpretation of the shaman voyager. Storyteller Johnny Qummun Ruben tells of the voyage:

> A powerful shaman has decided to prove to the people in his village that he can travel to the moon and back. They go about building a snowhouse with the shaman's instructions. He is weighed down with stones and sits in the very dark igloo. He tells the people to watch 3 stars in the night sky until they become parallel. Then it's time for them to open up the igloo. . . . The shaman has returned from the moon, looking very frosted and holding white translucent stones to prove he has been to the moon. He tells people that the moon is a cold, barren place and that no human life exists there. Having completed this rare feat, the people in the village hold him in high respect, and feed him well after his long journey. (*The Storytellers*, The Koffler Gallery, 1988)

The connection between the real and the mystical, Earth and the other-worldly, land and heaven are all told in the compelling visual stories of David Ruben Piqtoukun. The shaman (or *angako*), who is featured as the primary character in this innovative and powerful sculpture, unites these natural and supernatural worlds.

Illustrating the final part of this story in this work, David depicts the shaman at the moment he returns to Earth. His eyes are still closed, and he holds the moonstones in his outstretched hands for all to see. His legs are still tied down with heavy rocks in an attempt to hold the

Shaman Returning from the Moon
Stone with chalk and sinew, 26.5 x 36.0 x 17.0 cm

Shaman (reverse)

shaman's physical body to Earth while his soul travelled. A large disc attached to the back of the shaman's head represents the moon.

Although David is inspired by legends of the past, his interpretation is anchored in the present. Traditional stone carving techniques are combined with a broad collection of materials and textures found in and beyond the Arctic: Brazilian soapstone, caribou *sinew*, and Italian alabaster. David's work exists, in his own words, *between two worlds* – between the traditional Inuit culture of his past and the new society in which he lives.

SHAMAN

In Inuit society, the shaman was an important figure who acted as an adviser, doctor, and healer. Shamans could be either men or women. Most significantly, shamans helped Inuit connect with the spirit world – bringing together the worlds of humans and animals and ensuring a sense of oneness with nature.

SINEW

Sinew is made from animal tendon, which is a tough, fibrous material that connects muscle to bone. Sinew from animals such as caribou was commonly used by Inuit as thread and cording. In medieval times, sinew was used as a type of elastic.

INUKSHUK

In May 1987, David constructed an Inukshuk on the McMichael grounds. An Inukshuk (singular) is a stone figure traditionally built by the Inuit as a land marker. Translated into English as "likeness of a person," Inuksuit (plural) were built in many forms for several purposes, such as indicating the safest route, as a warning sign for danger, and to point out the location for good hunting or fishing. Inuksuit were also built as a memorial to show respect to a beloved person. An Inukshuk in the shape of a human is referred to as an Inunguak.

KENOJUAK ASHEVAK

FLOWER

BIRD

Many are the thoughts that rush over me, like the wings of birds out of darkness.

Kenojuak Ashevak in the film *Eskimo Artist Kenojuak*, 1963

KENOJUAK ASHEVAK (E7-1035)

Kenojuak Ashevak was born in an igloo on October 3, 1927, at Camp Ikerrasak, about 150 kilometres (93 miles) east of Kinngait (Cape Dorset) on Baffin Island. She was named after her mother's father and grew up in various summer and winter camps as her family migrated with the change in seasons. She never went to school, as at the time Inuit children learned the necessary survival skills from their elders. Kenojuak did not have an easy life and endured many hardships.

At the age of nineteen, Kenojuak entered into an arranged marriage with Johnniebo. Within the first few years of marriage, she had two children, Jamasie and Mary. When Kenojuak was in her mid-twenties, she became very ill with tuberculosis. Before leaving for treatment, Kenojuak gave birth to a third child, a boy she named Qiqituk. As there would be no one to care properly for the child while she was in the hospital, Kenojuak and Johnniebo adopted him out to another Inuit family. (Adoption in this manner was a very common occurrence, and Kenojuak and Johnniebo would later adopt four children themselves.) Qiqituk died shortly after during a measles epidemic.

Kenojuak was sent to a hospital in Quebec City, where she remained for almost four years. While being treated, Kenojuak began making dolls and beadwork, which were sold through the hospital. Kenojuak had learned traditional sewing techniques such as appliqué design from her beloved grandmother while she was growing up. After spending a year and a half in hospital, Kenojuak received the terrible news that her two older children had died. Jamasie had died after eating infected walrus meat and Mary died a few months later after becoming ill. Kenojuak had fourteen children in total, seven of whom died during childhood.

Kenojuak and Johnniebo moved to Kinngait in 1966 while she was expecting another child. The decision to leave the camp was a difficult

Flower Bird
Stonecut on paper, 61.8 x 86.0 cm

but necessary one. By the end of the 1960s, most Inuit had abandoned their traditional camps and moved to the settlements.

In the summer of 1955, Kenojuak began making sealskin and beaded works for sale through a program set up by Alma Houston, James Houston's wife. Kenojuak then started to experiment with drawing – the first woman in Kinngait to do so. Her first print was based on her design for an appliqué for a sealskin bag. It appeared in *Eskimo Graphic Art*, the first annual Cape Dorset Prints catalogue, in 1959.

Kenojuak's keen sense of design and composition has made her one of the best-known Inuit artists of her time, and she has received numerous honours and awards. She was elected to the Royal Academy of Arts in 1974; was appointed a Companion to the Order of Canada in 1982; received an Aboriginal Achievement Award in 1995; and was inducted into Canada's Walk of Fame in 2001. Kenojuak continues to produce drawings that are used for prints, stained-glass windows, and even on postage stamps! Fresh, inventive, and uniquely her own, works by Kenojuak have come to be known and respected all over the world. Kenojuak currently lives and works in Kinngait.

FLOWER BIRD

Kenojuak's bird appears to be an owl, sprouting a complex arrangement of flowers, feathers, leaves, wings, and other bird species. Although animals play an important role in the lives of Inuit, Kenojuak's bird is not from the land or Inuit mythology. Perhaps inspired by her intimate connection and struggles with the land, nature, and animal life, the *Flower Bird* is born from Kenojuak's vivid artistic imagination.

> I just take these things out of my thoughts and out of my imagination, and I don't really give any weight to the idea of its being an image of something. . . . I am just concentrating on placing it down on paper in a way that is pleasing to my own eye, whether it has anything to do with subjective reality or not.
> (Kenojuak Ashevak in *Kenojuak*, 1985)

Original drawing

Indeed, Kenojuak's birds are unique – this image of the bird magically unfolds before our eyes. The owl's physical attributes are exaggerated, embellished, and elaborated as Kenojuak cleverly captures the soul and energy of the bird spirit. Her complex composition with one central subject is enhanced and balanced by her fluid lines and choice of colour. As with so many artists of her generation, Kenojuak's artistic practice is connected to her work on everyday objects.

> I do not really consider myself a drawer, or an artist, or a sculptress, or whatever. I wouldn't say that of myself except in conjunction with the other things that I do. I would say, well yes, I draw and I sculpt, and I do appliqué, embroidery, and needlepoint. . . . I don't put any aspect of my experience first as the main thing. Being able to do embroidery and being able to go out on the land and all those other things are not secondary to being an artist. (Kenojuak Ashevak in *Kenojuak*, 1985)

Kenojuak's memories and experiences of the land, the animals, the culture, and the people ultimately find artistic expression through her rich imagination and considerable artistic skills. Her bold, emblematic images continue to remind Canadians and the world of her unique and enchanting vision.

Transferring the design

Carving the stone

The print stone

Stonecut Print (Printed by Timothy Ottochie)

Stonecut printing is an adaptation of woodblock printing. Large, fist-thick slabs of rock are evened out and polished, leaving a smooth, flat surface, which is painted white. The printmaker then traces a reverse image of the artist's drawing onto the stone with the use of carbon paper, and the resulting lines are darkened with ink. Using a chisel, the printmaker carves out areas that are not to be part of the printed image, leaving a raised surface. Ink is applied on the stone with a roller in layers starting with lighter shades and finishing with the darker ones. This process can often take more than an hour. Once the surface has been inked, a protective sheet is placed over the areas that are not part of the print and then the printing paper is placed on top. Only soft rice paper can be used, as the paper needs to be able to absorb the ink. A second protective sheet of paper is placed on top and the area is rubbed by hand, which transfers the ink to the paper. The paper is then peeled off of the stone and hung up to dry. Voila, one print! The process is then repeated to produce additional prints.

What Are Those Symbols at the Bottom of the Print?

These marks identify the artist, printmaker, and region where the print was made. The artist's mark in syllabics appears first, followed by that of the printmaker. The bottom symbol represents the community – the igloo symbol tells us that this print is from Cape Dorset. The symbol used in Cape Dorset today is that of the West Baffin Eskimo Co-operative. In 1974, the artist's mark was replaced by his or her name signed in syllabics along the bottom edge with other handwritten information, including the title of the work, method, and number in the edition. An edition is made up of a number of prints that are produced from the same stone. It is customary to record the number of the print above the total number of prints in the edition. The earliest prints were done in an edition of thirty, but fifty is now the standard number.

Why Does the Print Look Different from the Drawing?

Printmaking is a collaborative effort between the artist and the printmaker. While the artist draws the original design, it is up to the printmaker to determine how the work will be translated onto the stone. As we can see in this example, the printmaker (Timothy Ottochie) stayed very true to Kenojuak's design in terms of placement and line. When it came time to ink the stone, he chose softer colours, which changed the overall composition. While Kenojuak was not directly involved with the printing process, she would have seen early proofs and given her approval before the full edition was printed.

KENOJUAK'S FIRST PRINT

The bag at bottom right was used as the design for Kenojuak's first print, *Rabbit Eating Seaweed,* below (1959, stencil on paper, 23.1 x 61.1 cm).

Inking the stone

Rubbing the print

Pulling the print

Sealskin bag

I have a style of drawing that doesn't belong to anybody but me. It is my own and I own it and people can try to copy it but they can't. They try but they can't.

Kenojuak Ashevak in *Kenojuak*, 1985

TALELAYU OPIITLU (Stonecut Print, Printed by Saggiaktok Saggiaktok)

Talelayu Opiitlu means "sea goddess" and "owl" in English. The legend of the sea goddess is one of the most important among Inuit. Known as Talelayu (or more commonly as Sedna), she was believed to be a spirit who lived under the sea and ruled all creatures. Sedna was respected and feared because she controlled the results of the hunt, which Inuit relied upon for survival. Many have claimed to have seen her, including Kenojuak herself, who saw Sedna's face in the icy water.

Kenojuak's *Talelayu* combines the past with the present. It is a self-portrait of the artist expressing an important mythic spirit of the past – the sea goddess Talelayu. In the North, the natural universe (including the origins of humans, forces of nature, and human/animal

Kiawak Ashoona, *Sedna; Two Tails*
Stone, 37.5 x 71.3 x 11.0 cm

Talelayu Opiitlu
Stonecut and stencil on paper, 61.3 x 68.5 cm

Martha Anowtalik, *Sedna*
Stone and musk-ox hair
13.5 x 12.2 x 12.9 cm

behaviour) is often explained through Inuit legends and myths. Although these stories are part of an important Inuit oral tradition passed down from generation to generation, Kenojuak's artwork now becomes a visual representation of one of the North's most important mythic spirits.

Once in times long past people left the settlement at Quigmertoq in Sherman Inlet. They were going to cross the water and had made rafts of kayaks tied together. They were many and were in haste to get away to new hunting grounds. And there was not much room on the rafts they tied together.

At the village there was a little girl whose name was Nuliajuk. She jumped out on the raft, together with the other boys and girls, but no one cared about her, no one was related to her, and so they seized her and threw her into the water. In vain she tried to get hold of the edge of the raft; they cut her fingers off, and lo! As she sank to the bottom the stumps of her fingers became alive in the water and bobbed up round the raft like seals. That was how the seals came. But Nuliajuk herself sank to the bottom of the sea. There she became a spirit, the sea spirit, and she became the mother of the sea beasts, because the seals had formed out of her fingers that were cut off. And she also became mistress of everything else alive, the land beasts, too, that mankind had to hunt. (Rasmussen, Knud. "The Netsilik Eskimos," *Report of the Fifth Thule Expedition 1921–24*, Vol. VIII. Copenhagen, 1931: 190–443.)

LOCATED IN KLEINBURG, ONTARIO, the McMichael Canadian Art Collection is situated amid one hundred acres of serene conservation land and housed in a sprawling complex of intimate galleries built of fieldstone and hand-hewn logs. The McMichael offers a unique experience for discovering Canada through its art, peoples, cultures, and history. Renowned for its collection of paintings by Canada's most famous artists, the Group of Seven, the gallery's permanent collection also includes works by other well-known Canadians, including First Nations, Inuit, and contemporary artists.

ARTWORK CREDITS

page 9
Oviloo Tunnillie (b. 1949)
Woman Quarrying Stone 1998
Korok Inlet serpentinite
55.0 x 22.0 x 45.5 cm
Gift of Mr. Norman Yeager in memory of his wife,
Bess Yeager, 1926–1999
McMichael Canadian Art Collection
1999.8.1

page 15
Joe Talirunili (1893–1976)
The Migration 1976
Stone and sealskin with wood
32.5 x 42.0 x 23.0 cm
Purchase 1980
McMichael Canadian Art Collection
1980.2

page 21
Jessie Oonark (1906–1985)
Untitled date unknown
Wool, felt, embroidery thread, and thread
120.2 x 130.3 cm
Gift of Sam and Esther Sarick
McMichael Canadian Art Collection
1977.43

page 24
Pitseolak Ashoona (1904–1983)
Playing on the Igloo 1981
Printed by Timothy Ottochie (1904–1982)
Stonecut and stencil on paper
43.7 x 63.9 cm
Collection of the West Baffin Eskimo Co-operative Ltd.,
on loan to the McMichael Canadian Art Collection
CDP.27.15.1

page 27
Lukta Qiatsuk (1928–2004)
Owl Spirit 1987
Whalebone
46.0 x 156.8 x 103.5 cm
Gift of the West Baffin Eskimo Co-operative Ltd.
McMichael Canadian Art Collection
1989.8

pages 31 and 32
David Ruben Piqtoukun (b. 1950)
Alliok 1984
Stone with bone and teeth
38.0 x 39.0 x 11.5 cm
Purchase 1986
McMichael Canadian Art Collection
1986.29

pages 35 and 36
David Ruben Piqtoukun (b. 1950)
Shaman Returning from the Moon 1984
Stone with chalk and sinew
26.5 x 36.0 x 17.0 cm
Purchased with funds donated by Mr. Irwin Bernick
McMichael Canadian Art Collection
1986.47.A-.D

page 39
Kenojuak Ashevak (b. 1927)
Flower Bird
Stonecut on paper
Printed by Timothy Ottochie (1904–1982)
61.8 x 86.0 cm
Collection of the West Baffin Eskimo Co-operative Ltd.,
on loan to the McMichael Canadian Art Collection
CDP.40.126.1

page 41
Kenojuak Ashevak (b. 1927)
Drawing for print Flower Bird 1966–1976
Felt-tip pen on paper
50.8 x 66.5 cm
Collection of the West Baffin Eskimo Co-operative Ltd.,
on loan to the McMichael Canadian Art Collection
CD.40.825

page 42
Kenojuak Ashevak (b. 1927)
Print Stone for Flower Bird
Stone
Collection of the West Baffin Eskimo Co-operative Ltd.,
on loan to the McMichael Canadian Art Collection
CDL.1999.1

page 43 and page i
Kenojuak Ashevak (b. 1927)
Rabbit Eating Seaweed 1959
Printed by Iyola Kingwatsiak (1933–2000)
Stencil on paper
23.1 x 61.1 cm
Collection of the West Baffin Eskimo Co-operative Ltd.,
on loan to the McMichael Canadian Art Collection
CDP.40.12.2

page 44
Kiawak Ashoona (b. 1933)
Sedna; Two Tails 1989–1990
Stone
37.5 x 71.3 x 11.0 cm
Collection of the West Baffin Eskimo Co-operative Ltd.,
on loan to the McMichael Canadian Art Collection
J0587

page 45 and cover
Kenojuak Ashevak (b. 1927)
Talelayu Opiitlu 1979
Printed by Saggiaktok Saggiaktok
Stonecut and stencil on paper
61.3 x 68.5 cm
Collection of the West Baffin Eskimo Co-operative Ltd.,
on loan to the McMichael Canadian Art Collection
CDP.40.157.1

page 46
Martha Anowtalik (b. 1928)
Sedna
Stone and musk-ox hair
13.5 x 12.2 x 12.9 cm
Gift of Carol Heppenstall
McMichael Canadian Art Collection
1999.12.10

PHOTO CREDITS

Page 8
Oviloo Tunnillie.
Photo by John Reeves.

Page 11
Quarrying at Tatsiituq in Aberdeen Bay, 1963.
Photo by Terry Ryan.

Page 12 (top)
Kenojuak carving in tent, Cape Dorset, 1983.
Photo by Jimmy Manning.

Page 12 (middle)
Pauta Saila carving, 1968. Photo by / Gift of Norman E.
Hallendy. McMichael Canadian Art Collection Archives.

Page 12 (bottom)
Abraham Etungat, Cape Dorset, 1982.
Photo by John Reeves.

Page 14
Joe Talirunili.
Photo by Eugene Kedl.

Page 17
About to abandon the igloo village, the Eskimos load all
their household gear in their sleds, 1931, R.S. Finnie/
Library and Archives Canada/PA101188.

Page 18
Eskimos in Boat, Hudson Bay, N.W.T., Photographer:
A.P. Low, 1897. Photo 18690, Reproduced with the
Permission of the Minister of Public Works and
Government Services Canada, 2006 and Courtesy of
Natural Resources Canada, Geological survey of Canada.

Page 18
14¢ *Migration*, 1978, based on
The Migration by Joe Talirunili
© Canada Post Corporation 1978.
Reproduced with Permission.

Page 19
Robert Flaherty (1884–1951), *Nanook. The
Grammophone*. Allakariallak [Nanook] at Inukjuak post
with record player, 1920–1921 from the film *Nanook
of the North*. Photo reproduction from original vintage
photogravure N370, Robert and Frances Flaherty Study
Centre at Claremont (FSCC).

Page 20
Jessie Oonark.
Photo by John Reeves.

Page 22
Jessie Oonark at home sewing, Baker Lake, c.1973.
Photo by Jack Butler.

Page 23
Woman using ulu, South West Baffin Island, 1980.
Photo by / Gift of Norman E. Hallendy. McMichael
Canadian Art Collection Archives.

Page 24 (bottom)
Qarmaq 1, 1997. Photo by Dr. Ansgar Walk.

Page 25 (top)
Three Inuit girls in front of a tent, Health Canada /
Library and Archives Canada/e002394407.

Page 25 (bottom)
Cape Dorset, 1973. Photo by / Gift of Norman E.
Hallendy. McMichael Canadian Art Collection Archives.

Page 26
Lukta Qiatsuk, 1991. Photo by Jean Blodgett.
McMichael Canadian Art Collection Archives.

Page 26
45¢ *Mother and Child*, 1990, based on *Mother and
Child*, c.1969 by Lukta Qiatsuk © Canada Post
Corporation 1990. Reproduced with Permission.

Page 28 (top)
Toni Onley standing behind whalebone on Nottingham
Island. Photo courtesy of the Toni Onley Archives.

Page 28 (middle, bottom)
Lukta Qiatsuk carving *Owl Spirit*, 1987.
McMichael Canadian Art Collection.

Page 29
Bowhead whale illustration by Charles Douglas,
courtesy of the Canadian Museum of Nature, Ottawa,
Canada.

Page 30
David Ruben Piqtoukun, 1990.
Photo by / Gift of Esther E. Atkin.
McMichael Canadian Art Collection Archives.

Page 37
David Ruben Piqtoukun building the Inukshuk at the
McMichael Gallery, 1987. McMichael Canadian Art
Collection Archives.

Page 38
Kenojuak Ashevak.
Photo by Leslie Boyd Ryan.

Page 40
6¢ *Centennial of the Northwest Territories*, 1970, based
on *The Enchanted Owl*, 1960 by Kenojuak Ashevak, ©
Canada Post Corporation 1970. Reproduced with
Permission.

Page 41
Kenojuak Ashevak drawing in her home, Cape Dorset,
1983.
Photo by Jimmy Manning.

Page 42 (top)
Timothy Ottochie transferring design, 1982.
Photo by John Reeves.

Page 42 (middle)
Timothy Ottochie cutting stone block, 1968.
Photo by / Gift of Norman E. Hallendy. McMichael
Canadian Art Collection Archives.

Page 43 (top)
Lukta Qiatsuk inking print stone, 1983.
Photo by Jimmy Manning.
Courtesy of Dorset Fine Arts.

Page 43 (second from top)
Iyola Kingwatsiak rubbing stonecut print, Cape Dorset,
1968.
Photo by / Gift of Norman E. Hallendy.
McMichael Canadian Art Collection Archives.

Page 43 (third from top)
Pulling a stonecut print, 1978.
Photo by M. Jackson,
Indian and Northern Affairs Canada.

Page 43 (bottom)
Sealskin handbag made by Kenojuak in the early 1950s.
Photo by Bert Beaver.
Courtesy of Dorset Fine Arts.

SELECTED BIBLIOGRAPHY

Biography of Jessie Oonark, compiled by The Canadian Eskimo Arts Council, 1971.

Blodgett, Jean. *Kenojuak*. Toronto: Firefly Books, 1985.

Brett Davis, David Ruben Piqtoukun: *Contemporary Age of Bronze and Stone*
(Exhibition Pamphlet). Toronto: Canadian Sculpture Centre, 2000.

Feeney, John. *Eskimo Artist Kenojuak* (Film). Ottawa: National Film Board of Canada,
1963.

Gustavison, Susan. *Northern Rock: Contemporary Inuit Stone Sculpture*. Kleinburg:
McMichael Canadian Art Collection, 1999.

Leroux, Odette, Marion E. Jackson, and Minnie Aodla Freeman, eds. *Inuit Women Artists*.
Vancouver: Douglas & McIntyre; Ottawa: Canadian Museum of Civilization, 1994.

Joe Talirunili: A Grace Beyond the Reach of Art. Montreal: La Federation des cooperatives
du Nouveau-Quebec, 1977.

The Storytellers: Sculptures by David Ruben Piqtoukun, Photographs by Tom Skudra
(Exhibition Catalogue). North York: The Koffler Gallery, 1988.

Wight, Darlene. *Out of Tradition: Abraham Anghik/David Ruben Piqtoukun*. Winnipeg:
Winnipeg Art Gallery, 1989.